A **TRUE**

NERVOUS SYSTEM

Jenny Mason

Children's Press®
An imprint of Scholastic Inc.

Content Consultant
Madison Chisholm, BSc (Hons), MSc Bioscience
The University of Winnipeg

Library of Congress Cataloging-in-Publication Data available
ISBN 978-1-339-02105-8 (library binding) | ISBN 978-1-339-02106-5 (paperback)

10 9 8 7 6 5 4 3 2 1   24 25 26 27 28

Printed in China 62
First edition, 2024

Design by Kathleen Petelinsek
Series produced by Spooky Cheetah Press

Find the Truth!

Everything you are about to read is true *except* for one of the sentences on this page.

Which one is **TRUE**?

T or F   Brains wrinkle with age, just like skin.

T or F   People and animals need stress to escape from danger.

Find the answers in this book.

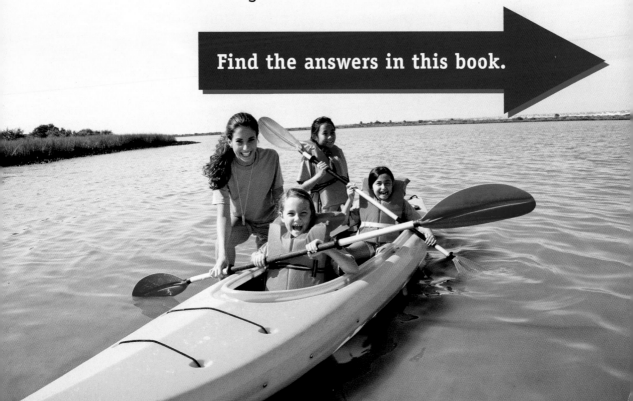

What's in This Book?

The **BIG** Truth

Your central
nervous system
contains billions
of nerve cells.

Teamwork!

Your brain is made up of many parts.

3 Problems with the Nervous System

Your brain is inside your skull. It is important to keep it safe from injury.

INTRODUCTION

You **learn** to ride a bike. You **laugh** at jokes. You **feel** the zing of frosty air or the sizzle of the sun. You **think**. You **remember**. None of these experiences would be possible without your nervous system. All animals have a nervous system. Zebras. Bees. Even jellyfish. The nervous system directs everything you think, feel, and do. All parts of your body use your nervous system to **communicate** with one another—and **it never stops** to rest. However, most of the time, you don't notice it doing any work.

The nervous system is made up of the **peripheral** nervous system (PNS) and the central nervous system (CNS). These two systems work together to make you—you. Read on to learn more about this amazing body system.

The nervous system creates your every thought, feeling, and action.

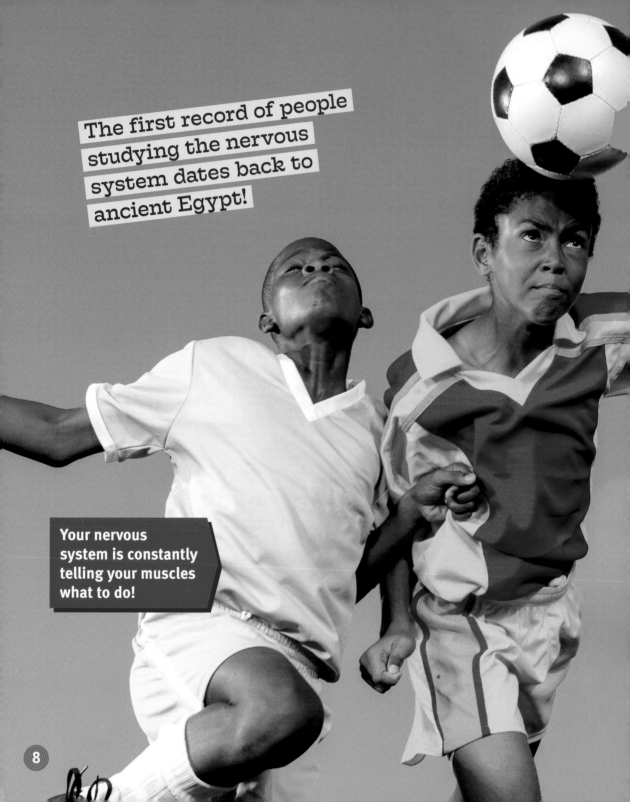

The first record of people studying the nervous system dates back to ancient Egypt!

Your nervous system is constantly telling your muscles what to do!

Sensing and Doing

Let's look at your peripheral nervous system first.
It has two jobs. First, it senses things. For that,
the PNS relies on your five **senses**: sight,
hearing, touch, smell, and taste. Your eyes, ears,
skin, nose, and mouth constantly gather
information about the world around you. The PNS
also makes your body do things. It tells your
muscles when and how to move. The PNS also
keeps your heart, stomach, lungs, and other
organs working to keep you alive.

The Right Tool for the Job

Nerve **cells** are the most important tools in the nervous system, and your body and brain contain billions of them. A single nerve cell is called a neuron [NEW-rahn]. It has three basic parts: a cell body, branches called dendrites [DEN-drites], and a single axon [AK-sahn]. Dendrites receive signals and axons send signals. Signals can come from your senses. Sniffing a flower and licking an ice-cream cone create signals. Movements create signals too. Even your **emotions** pass through neurons as signals.

Parts of a Neuron

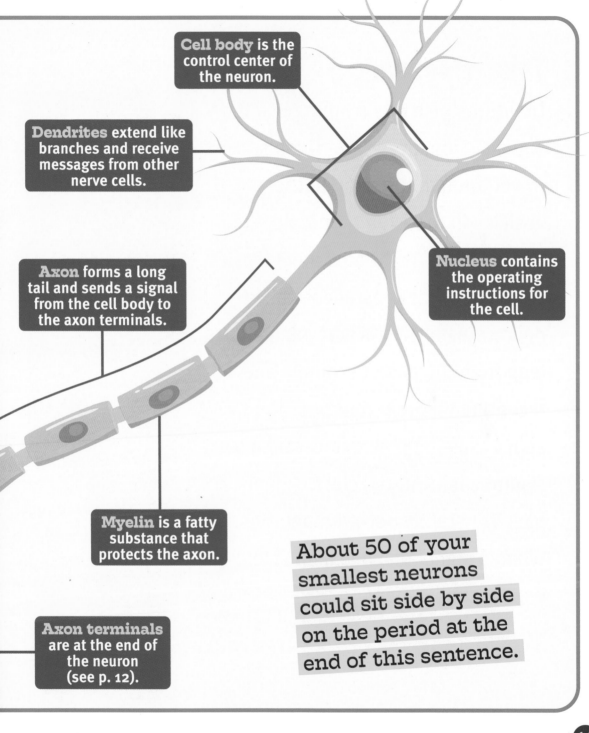

Cell body is the control center of the neuron.

Dendrites extend like branches and receive messages from other nerve cells.

Nucleus contains the operating instructions for the cell.

Axon forms a long tail and sends a signal from the cell body to the axon terminals.

Myelin is a fatty substance that protects the axon.

Axon terminals are at the end of the neuron (see p. 12).

About 50 of your smallest neurons could sit side by side on the period at the end of this sentence.

Take a Message

Dendrites pick up incoming electric signals. From there, the signals travel through the axon to the vesicles in the axon terminals. The vesicles are little pockets that store chemical substances called neurotransmitters. Neurotransmitters leap from the axon terminals to receptors on other neurons. The space they jump across is called a synaptic [si-NAP-tik] **cleft**. Signals pass constantly between neurons. When a signal reaches a muscle, it sparks movement.

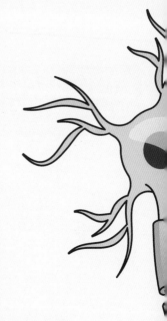

Sending a Message

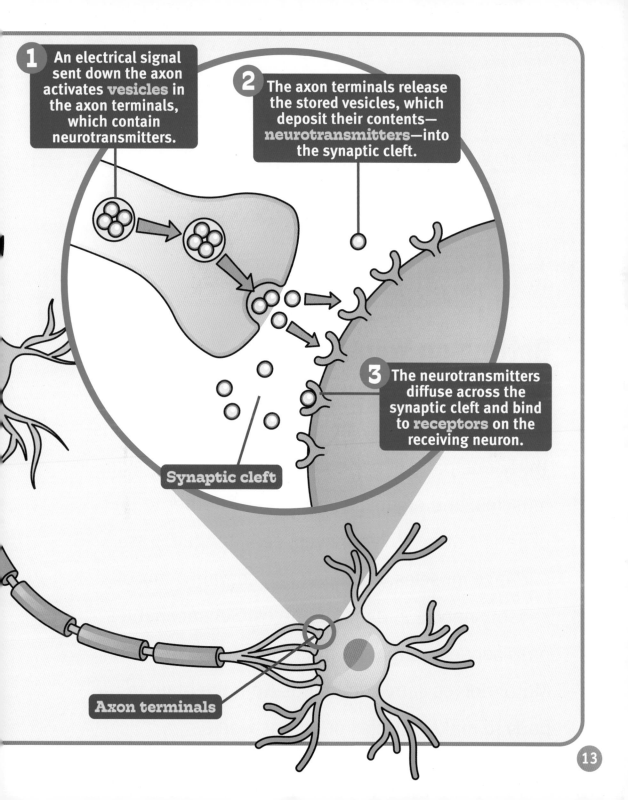

1 An electrical signal sent down the axon activates vesicles in the axon terminals, which contain neurotransmitters.

2 The axon terminals release the stored vesicles, which deposit their contents—neurotransmitters—into the synaptic cleft.

3 The neurotransmitters diffuse across the synaptic cleft and bind to receptors on the receiving neuron.

Synaptic cleft

Axon terminals

Getting on Your Nerves

Nerves carry signals back and forth between your body and brain. They are made of bundles of axons. Thirty-one pairs of nerves extend through the skin, muscles, and organs in your body. Another 12 pairs of nerves attach to your eyes, ears, tongue, nose, and face muscles. Each pair can contain a mix of sensory nerves and motor nerves. Sensory nerves pass sense information from the body to the brain. Motor nerves carry commands from the brain to the body to make muscles or organs work.

What Are Reflexes?

It's a sizzling summer day. Your family is driving to a lake. You reach for the seatbelt and— OUCH! The metal latch burns your fingertips. You jerk away without a thought. That jerk is a reflex. Reflexes are fast movements.

They come from rapid signals between sensory and motor nerves. They do not involve your brain. Reflexes protect us. Your sneeze and cough reflexes clear out your airways. The flinching reflex protects our eyes.

Your funny bone is actually a nerve in your elbow. A doctor might check your reflexes by tapping that spot.

We are born with most of our reflex actions.

We blink up to 19,200 times per day. That's your autonomic nervous system at work!

The ANS works behind the scenes to keep you alive.

ANS: Your Inner Robot

Lub-dub, lub-dub. That is the steady rhythm of your heartbeat. It operates automatically like a robot. You never have to think about it. That is because your PNS has a special set of nerves that control the most important motor commands sent to your organs. These nerves belong to the autonomic nervous system (ANS). The ANS manages body functions in the background. Your heartbeat, breathing, and digestion are good examples. These actions happen automatically, even when you sleep.

SNS: Just Do It

Can you wiggle your toes? If you can, your somatic nervous system (SNS) is working. The nerves of the SNS are in charge of any bodily actions you choose to do. These are **voluntary** actions.

The SNS can control some ANS jobs too. Try this experiment: Hold your breath for 10 seconds. When you choose not to breathe, your SNS controls the ANS. This takeover is usually brief. Imagine if you forgot to breathe!

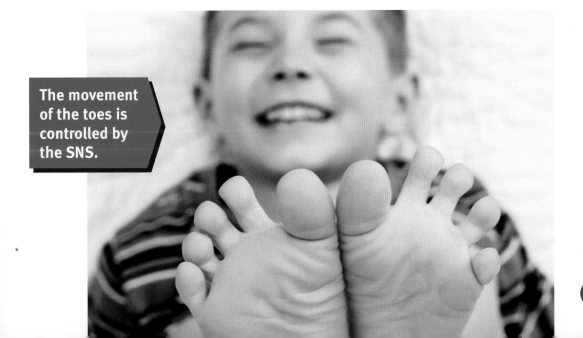

The movement of the toes is controlled by the SNS.

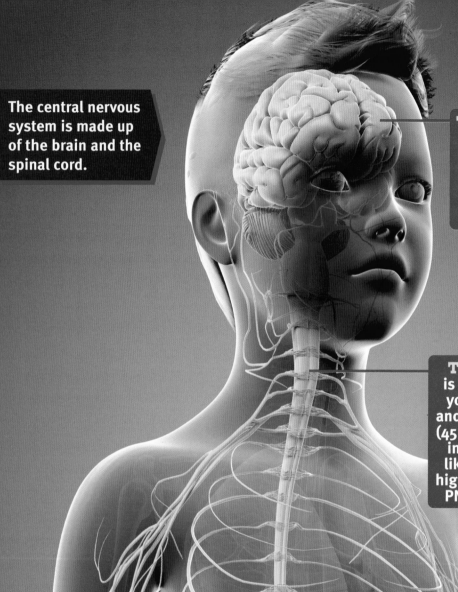

The central nervous system is made up of the brain and the spinal cord.

The brain weighs about 3 pounds (1.4 kilograms) on average. Signals fly in and out of your brain and scatter across it.

The spinal cord is about as thick as your pinkie finger, and around 18 inches (45 centimeters) long in adults. It works like an information highway between the PNS and the brain.

Electrical impulses in your brain travel at speeds of up to 268 miles (431 kilometers) per hour.

Signals In, Signals Out

The brain and the spinal cord make up the central nervous system (CNS). The spinal cord sends what the body senses to the brain. The brain is packed with billions of neurons that receive this information. In response they fire 5 to 50 signals every second! Those signals create your thoughts, feelings, and memories. They also trigger actions that are relayed by the spinal cord and the PNS to the body's muscles, making your body move.

Protection for the CNS

The spinal cord is made up of a long bundle of neurons. It nests inside your backbone. Your backbone is made of 33 stacked bones called vertebrae [ver-tuh-BRAY] that protect the spinal cord. The backbone extends from the pelvis to the skull. The skull is made of several different bones. It protects your brain.

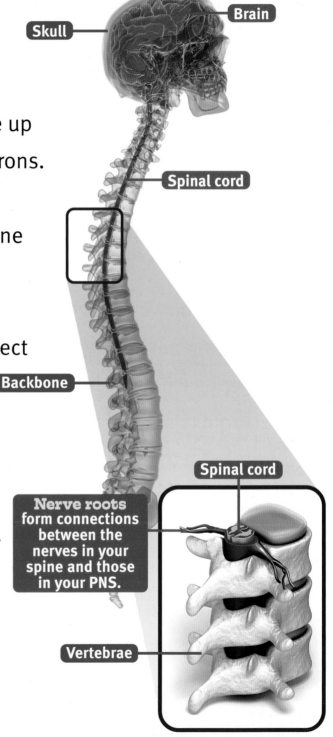

Skull

Brain

Spinal cord

Backbone

Nerve roots form connections between the nerves in your spine and those in your PNS.

Spinal cord

Vertebrae

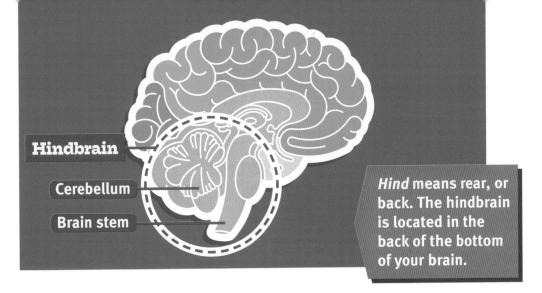

Hindbrain

Cerebellum

Brain stem

Hind means rear, or back. The hindbrain is located in the back of the bottom of your brain.

Where Brain and Body Connect

The spinal cord plugs into the bottom of the brain, also called the hindbrain. This area is in charge of your autonomic nervous system. It commands all your robotic functions like breathing, heartbeat, and balance. The hindbrain includes a large portion of the brain stem and the cerebellum. Special clusters of nerve fibers form the brain stem. Cerebellum means "little brain." It is found near the back of your head. It takes care of tricky movements like drawing, using scissors, or tying shoelaces.

The Inner Brain

The inner brain sits on top of the brain stem. It is packed with clustered neurons that specialize in certain jobs. One important cluster is the thalamus [THA-luh-mus]. Almost all sensory and motor signals pass through the thalamus. It directs signals to particular areas of the brain and the body. Large clusters of neurons called basal ganglia [BAY-suhl GANG-lee-uh] wrap around the thalamus. Without basal ganglia, your muscles would twitch or flail all the time.

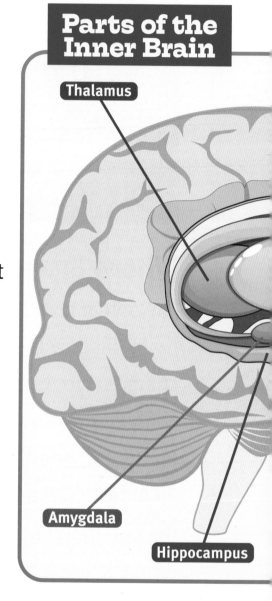

Parts of the Inner Brain

Thalamus

Amygdala

Hippocampus

The olfactory nerve sends the sense of smell directly into the brain.

22

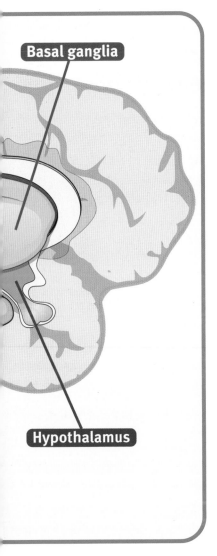

Basal ganglia

Hypothalamus

Feelings and Memory

The inner brain also contains the hypothalamus [HY-poh-tha-luh-mus]. Among other things, the hypothalamus wakes you from sleep and lets you know when you are hungry or thirsty. It also instructs certain **glands** to release the chemicals that make you feel angry, happy, or nervous. The hippocampus [HIH-puh-cam-pus] is another important structure in the inner brain. When memories form, the hippocampus sends them to special storage areas in the brain. The amygdala [uh-MIG-duh-luh] is found here too. This structure triggers feelings of fear.

The Top Talent

The cerebrum is the biggest part of your brain. It covers the brain stem, cerebellum, and inner brain. The cerebrum is packed with neurons and fatty cells. It is the most highly developed part of the brain. And it is responsible for some of the most amazing tasks, like learning, thinking, planning, and imagining.

There is a lot that we still don't understand about how our brains work!

Timeline: Nervous System Discoveries

1543
Belgian anatomist Andreas Vesalius first diagrams the nervous system in detailed drawings of the brain and internal body systems.

1791
The discovery is made that electrical signals move through the nervous system.

1870s
Spanish scientist Santiago Ramón y Cajal creates the first accurate drawings of neurons. These drawings help show how the brain works.

1907
Cécile Vogt-Mugnier discovers that different regions of the brain have different roles. She and her husband, Oskar Vogt, are the first to map the cortex.

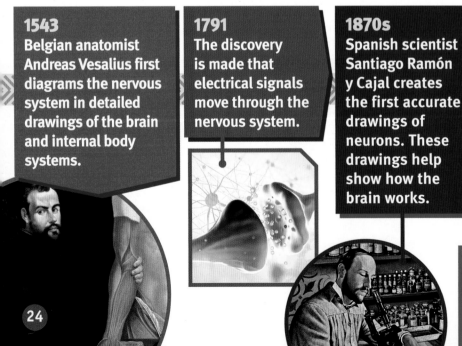

The Secret of the Wrinkles

The cortex is the wrinkly outer layer of the cerebrum. It is a large sheet of neurons and fatty **tissues**. Stretched flat, the cortex would be as big as a full page of a newspaper. It would not fit in your head. That is why it has grooves, folds, and wrinkles. The more neurons a brain has, the more it must bunch up and fold.

Every person has a unique wrinkle pattern on their cortex, like a fingerprint.

1972
Candace Pert, a biologist, discovers emotions are produced by chemical proteins called peptides.

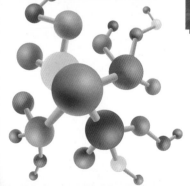

1990
Scientists Seiji Ogawa and Ken Kwong invent the functional magnetic resonance imaging (fMRI) technique. Researchers and doctors can observe a living brain while a person thinks, talks, or sleeps.

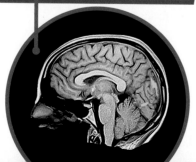

2016
A microchip replaces motor nerves for people with paralyzed arms. The chip, which is implanted in the brain, acts just like a neuron sending signals to move the arms.

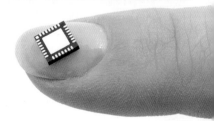

Two Brains Are Better Than One

The cerebrum is divided into two sections, or **hemispheres**. The left hemisphere controls the right side of the body. The right hemisphere controls the left side. Experts are not sure why the sides are swapped. Each hemisphere also houses different skills. The left hemisphere is great at math and languages. The right hemisphere can recognize faces. It processes music and daydreams.

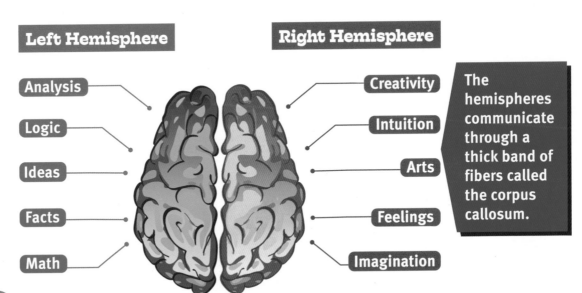

Left Hemisphere

- Analysis
- Logic
- Ideas
- Facts
- Math

Right Hemisphere

- Creativity
- Intuition
- Arts
- Feelings
- Imagination

The hemispheres communicate through a thick band of fibers called the corpus callosum.

Sleepy Head

Your brain and body need sleep. While you sleep, the nervous system is busy at work. It triggers glands to release chemicals that heal injured tissues. These substances also process any deep emotions you felt during the day. Sleeping gives the brain time to store memories like a music lesson or how to solve a tricky math problem.

Everyone dream about two hours night. Some pec dream in color. (see dreams in b and white.

Specialization

The hemispheres of your brain are divided into different areas called lobes. Lobes come in pairs, with one located on each hemisphere. Each lobe is packed with neurons that focus on specific jobs. This organized structure helps the brain work fast.

People with synesthesia taste sounds or hear colors. Sensory information triggers several of their brain lobes at the same time.

The Brain's Lobes

Parietal lobes process sensations like touch, temperature, pain, and taste. They also process reading and math.

Occipital lobes deal with vision. They merge the images seen from each of our eyes into one image.

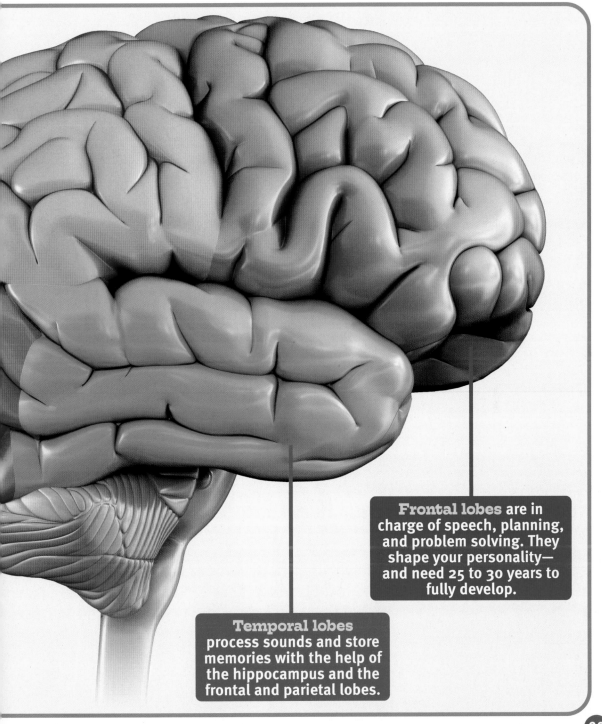

Frontal lobes are in charge of speech, planning, and problem solving. They shape your personality—and need 25 to 30 years to fully develop.

Temporal lobes process sounds and store memories with the help of the hippocampus and the frontal and parietal lobes.

Teamwork!

The nervous system does not function on its own. Find out how it works with other systems in your body to keep you running!

Respiratory System:

Your ANS is responsible for keeping your lungs breathing in and out, and your brain monitors your body's oxygen levels. In turn, your respiratory system supplies much needed oxygen to the brain. In fact, your brain uses 20 percent of the oxygen your body takes in. That's more than any other body system.

Muscular System:

Nerves in the nervous system command the muscles with electrical and chemical signals. Your nervous system is what gets you moving. The muscles of your organs pump, churn, and pulse because the nervous system tells them to.

Respiratory System

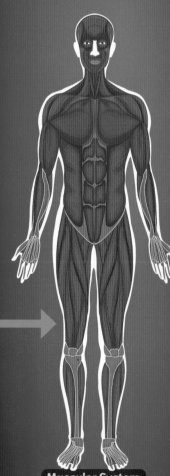

Muscular System

Circulatory System:

The ANS is what keeps your heart pumping the blood around your body 24 hours a day. The circulatory system delivers oxygen and nutrient-rich blood to all your systems—including the nervous system—and removes waste.

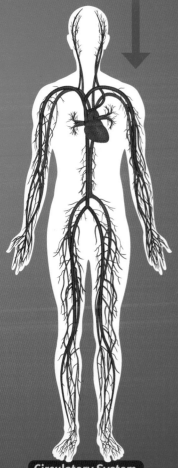

Circulatory System

Digestive System:

The brain checks to see if you are hungry or thirsty, and the ANS works with your digestive system to turn food into energy for your brain and body. The nervous system needs a lot of fuel because it never rests.

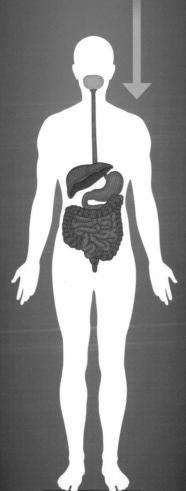

Digestive System

Skeletal System:

Sensory nerves in the PNS report any pains, aches, and breaks to the brain. The brain commands other systems to help grow, heal, and repair your bones. The bones of the skull and spine protect the brain and spinal cord.

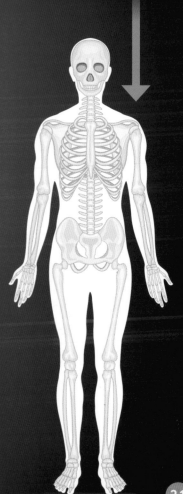

Skeletal System

Physical therapy can help some problems with the nervous system.

Your brain does not have any pain receptors. So it's not your brain that hurts with a headache. The pain in your head, face, or neck is misinterpreted as pain in your brain!

Problems with the Nervous System

It's the end of a rough school day. The bus ride home was noisy. Now your head aches. Headaches flare up when your nervous system is stressed. Muscles and nerves around the neck and head throb and hurt. Headaches are usually a brief problem. Other nervous system disorders can be very serious. Injuries, infections, and diseases can harm the PNS and the CNS. They can **paralyze** muscles. They dish out pain.

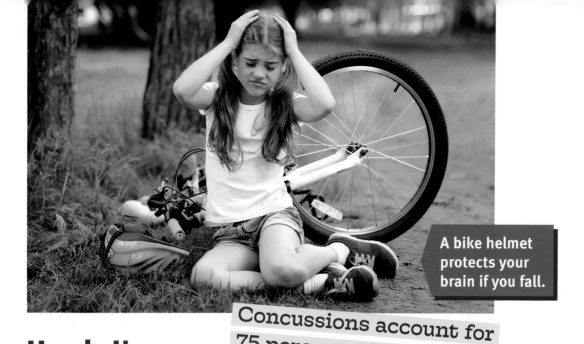

A bike helmet protects your brain if you fall.

Concussions account for 75 percent of all TBIs.

Heads Up

Bonk! A hit to the head can be a big deal. A hard impact can injure the brain. Doctors refer to a serious head injury as a traumatic brain injury (TBI). Concussions are the most common TBI. Whipping the head back and forth suddenly also causes concussions. The brain bounces or twists inside the skull. Brain tissues bruise, tear, and swell. Resting gives the brain time to heal. People with concussions should avoid bright lights and complex tasks for a few days.

Spinal Cord Injuries

The brain is not the only part of the CNS that can suffer injuries. Major accidents can injure the spinal cord. If the bones in the back break, they can slice into the cord. As a result, muscles below the cut cannot receive signals from the brain. They become frozen, or paralyzed. Other injuries pinch the cord. Muscles below the pinch receive patchy signals. They do not move as well. They may feel numb or tingle. Surgeries and medicines can treat these issues.

Seat belts protect your CNS—and can save your life!

Stress and Strain

Grades. Chores. Bullies. Daily life offers plenty of worries, which can strain the nervous system. Constant worry, or **anxiety**, damages neurons in the hippocampus, causing it to shrink. Glands stop producing "feel-good" chemicals. Instead, the amygdala releases "feel-fear" chemicals and worrying increases. The amygdala grows bigger. This cycle is known as a stress disorder—and lots of kids deal with it. Stress disorders can lead to anxiety and depression, so it is important to get help. Therapy can help. There are also medicines that are used to treat stress disorders.

Regular exercise and meditation can help people who feel anxious or overwhelmed.

Everyone feels anxious sometimes.

Designed to Stress

Stress feels awful—and yet, we cannot survive without it. Stress evolved to help humans and other animals escape or fight-off danger. It triggers your flight-or-fight response. Imagine a lion is about to pounce on you. Your autonomic nervous system instantly revs up your whole body. The brain dumps move-fast chemicals into the blood. Your heart races. Breathing speeds up. Digestion stops. Your mouth goes dry. These responses make you stronger and faster. They keep you alive. Stress is good in small doses.

Brilliant scientist Stephen Hawking lived with ALS for 55 years.

Physical therapy can help with MS symptoms.

Under Attack

Some diseases attack the nervous system. Multiple sclerosis (MS) is a disease that attacks the myelin on neurons. Damaged neurons cannot send signals to one another. People with MS have difficulties with movement, balance, and memory. Amyotrophic lateral sclerosis (ALS) is a disease that kills motor neurons over time. Muscles stop working. ALS eventually stops the heart and lungs. Medicines and special exercises can reduce some MS symptoms. ALS has no known cures.

Treasure Each Connection

Connections are at the heart of your nervous system. The body's PNS connects you to the world. Nerves connect what you feel to your CNS. Electrical and chemical signals connect the neurons throughout your brain. You have thoughts and emotions. You make memories. Signals shoot out to connect brain commands to the body. You may run or ride a bike. You read books and watch movies. You learn new skills. Life is a treasure chest of experiences thanks to the wonders of the nervous system.

Your nervous system helps you live life to the fullest!

Nervous System Care

Doctors, nurses, and therapists work with us to prevent and treat disease. Here are a few healthcare professionals who treat the nervous system, and some of the tests they may perform.

Reflex hammer

Pediatrician: Your regular doctor checks your nervous system by tapping your knee with a small hammer that has a rubber head. The hammer hits a nerve and triggers a reflex. Your leg kicks. Sticking out your tongue and wiggling your eyebrows test other nerves.

CT machine

Psychologist

Speech tools

Neurologist: This doctor uses special tests and equipment to find problems in the nervous system. For example, a neurologist can take pictures of the brain and body. The doctor might use a CT machine to create a picture of what the body looks like inside.

Psychologist: A psychologist treats conditions like stress, anxiety, and depression. In therapy sessions, doctors may ask many questions. They listen as a patient talks about troubling thoughts and worries. They coach people on how to handle stress or anxiety.

Speech/Language Pathologist: These doctors correct speech problems. Some nervous system disorders disrupt a person's ability to speak. They might stutter. They may have trouble making certain sounds, like "R" or "L." The pathologist has special tools that help patients make the right mouth shapes.

Take Care of Your Nervous System

Keeping your nervous system healthy is important. And if you take care of it now, you will have a healthier future. Here are five things that you can do to protect your nervous system health and more.

Eat Healthy Foods

The nervous system needs plenty of vitamins and minerals. Healthy fats protect nerve tissues and speed up signals. They boost your mood too. Make sure you eat plenty of leafy greens, nuts, and fish. Dark chocolate and berries are great snacks.

Get Plenty of Sleep

Your brain and body grow and heal tissues when you sleep. Toxins are cleared away too. Neurons store information while you rest. Children need 9–12 hours of sleep each night.

42

Enjoy Lots of Playtime

The networks of nerves and neurons in your brain and body grow stronger when you play. Playtime can be physical, like when you play tag. Playtime can also be mental, like when you solve puzzles.

Practice Healthy Ways to Worry Less

Use a weighted blanket to calm your PNS or shake your body when you feel anxious. Wiggle until you giggle. Finally, take a break. Why not go for a walk or meditate?

Spend Time with Your Family and Friends

Connecting with great people actually strengthens your brain. It releases special chemicals that nourish your brain cells and make you feel good.

True Statistics

The portion of blood in the body dedicated to the brain: 20 percent

Time you spend dreaming each night: 2 hours

Total time you will have spent sleeping by age 75: 25 years

Animal with the largest brain: The sperm whale, whose brain can weigh up to 20 pounds (9 kg)

Amount of time your brain can survive without oxygen: 4 to 6 minutes

Approximate percentage of kids in the United States suffering from anxiety or depression as of 2020: 13 percent

Approximate number of neurons in the human brain: 86 billion

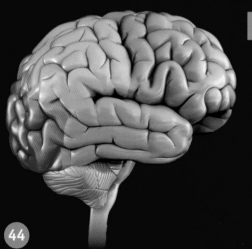

Did you find the truth?

F Brains wrinkle with age, just like skin.

T People and animals need stress to escape from danger.

Resources

Other books in this series:

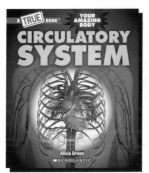

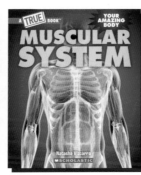
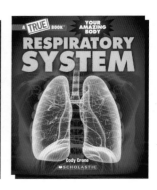

You can also look at:

Deak, JoAnn, Terrence Deak, and Neely Daggett. *Good Night to Your Fantastic Elastic Brain: A Growth Mindset Bedtime Book for Kids.* Naperville, IL: Sourcebooks Explore, 2022.

Green, Dan. *The Adventures of Your Brain.* New York, NY: Union Square Kids, 2017.

Lewis, Carrie. *All About Anxiety.* Minneapolis, MN: Beaming Books, 2020.

Pettiford, Rebecca. *The Nervous System.* Hopkins, MN: Bellwether Media, 2019.

Swanson, Jennifer. *Brain Games: The Mind-Blowing Science of Your Amazing Brain.* Washington, DC: National Geographic Kids, 2015.

Glossary

anxiety (ang-ZYE-i-tee) a feeling of worry or fear

cells (SELZ) the smallest units of an animal or a plant

cleft (KLEFT) a split or division

emotions (i-MOH-shunz) feelings, such as happiness, love, or anger

glands (GLANDZ) organs in the body that produce or release natural chemicals

hemispheres (HEM-i-sfeerz) each half of a round object

organs (OR-guhnz) parts of the body, such as the heart or the kidneys, that have a certain purpose

paralyze (PAR-uh-lize) to cause a loss of the power to move or feel a part of the body

peripheral (puh-RIF-ur-uhl) of or having to do with the outer part or edge of something

senses (SEN-sez) the five powers a living being uses to learn about its surroundings

tissues (TISH-ooz) masses of similar cells that form a particular part or organ of an animal or a plant

voluntary (VAH-luhn-ter-ee) controlled by the will

Index

Page numbers in **bold** indicate illustrations.

About the Author

Jenny Mason is a story-hunter. She explores foreign countries, canyon mazes, and burial crypts to gather the facts that make the best true tales. She'll interview NASA engineers or sniff a 200-year-old rotten skull. Her research knows no bounds! Jenny does martial arts and triathlons to keep her nervous system healthy. She received her MFA in Writing for Children and Young Adults from the Vermont College of Fine Arts. She also holds an MPhil from Trinity College Dublin. Find all of Jenny's books and projects at jynnemason.com.